PROTECTING THE NATION WITH THE U.S. AIR FORCE

Rescue and Prevention: Defending Our Nation

PROTECTING THE NATION WITH THE U.S. AIR FORCE

CHRIS McNAB

MASON CREST PUBLISHERS
www.masoncrest.com

Mason Crest Publishers Inc.
370 Reed Road
Broomall, PA 19008
(866) MCP-BOOK (toll free)
www.masoncrest.com

First printing

1 2 3 4 5 6 7 8 9 10

Library of Congress Cataloging-in-Publication Data on file
at the Library of Congress

ISBN 1-59084-416-5

Editorial and design by
Amber Books Ltd.
Bradley's Close
74–77 White Lion Street
London N1 9PF
www.amberbooks.co.uk

Project Editor: Michael Spilling
Design: Graham Curd
Picture Research: Natasha Jones

Printed and bound in Jordan

Picture credits
Amber Books: 13; TRH: 8, 11, 14, 16, 18, 20, 23, 24, 25, 26, 27, 30–31, 37, 38, 43, 44, 47,
48, 51, 52, 53, 55, 54, 58, 61, 62, 64, 65, 67, 68, 70, 73, 77, 78, 81, 83, 87, 88;
U.S. Department of Defense: 6, 19, 32, 34, 35, 41, 74.
Front cover: TRH, U.S. Department of Defense (bottom left).

DEDICATION

This book is dedicated to those who perished in the terrorist attacks of
September 11, 2001, and to all the committed individuals who continually
serve to defend freedom and protect the American people.

CONTENTS

INTRODUCTION

September 11, 2001, saw terrorism cast its lethal shadow across the globe. The deaths inflicted at the Twin Towers, at the Pentagon, and in Pennsylvania were truly an attack on the world and civilization itself. However, even as the impact echoed around the world, the forces of decency were fighting back: Americans drew inspiration from a new breed of previously unsung, everyday heroes. Amid the smoking rubble, firefighters, police officers, search-and-rescue, and other "first responders" made history. The sacrifices made that day will never be forgotten.

Out of the horror and destruction, we have fought back on every front. When the terrorists struck, their target was not just the United States, but also the values that the American people share with others all over the world who cherish freedom. Country by country, region by region, state by state, we have strengthened our public-safety efforts to make it much more difficult for terrorists.

Others have come to the forefront: from the Coast Guard to the Border Patrol, a wide range of agencies work day and night for our protection. Before the terrorist attacks of September 11, 2001, launched them into the spotlight, the courage of these guardians went largely unrecognized, although in truth, the sense of service was always honor enough for them. We can never repay the debt we owe them, but by increasing our understanding of the work they do, the *Rescue and Prevention: Defending Our Nation* books will enable us to better appreciate our brave defenders.

Steven L. Labov—CISM, MSO, CERT 3

Chief of Department, United States Search and Rescue Task Force

Left: A pilot climbs into the titanium-armored cockpit of an A-10 Thunderbolt, one of the USAF's main ground-attack aircraft.

HISTORY OF THE U.S. AIR FORCE

In 1997, the U.S. Air Force celebrated its 50th anniversary. Although it is one of the youngest elements of the U.S. military, it is the most potent air force in existence today.

In December 1903, the pioneers of powered flight, the Wright brothers, flew the first heavier-than-air aircraft, a **biplane** called the "Flier." The flight at the sands of Kitty Hawk, North Carolina, began the history of civil and military aviation and the history of the United States Air Force (USAF).

For military **tacticians**, aircraft offered the ability to cross enemy lines at will on either combat or reconnaissance missions. The U.S. Army Signal Corps, the branch of the Army concerned with communications and surveillance, formed the Aeronautical Division on August 1, 1907. In 1909, it received its first aircraft, a later version of the Wrights' Flier, and by 1913, the Army had a fully operational unit, the 1st Aero Squadron. However, military aviation was still young. The Army relied more on hot-air balloons and **airships** to conduct its reconnaissance, as it had done so since the Civil War (1861–1865) and the Spanish-American War (1889). It would take a world war to change this way of thinking.

Left: A USAF pilot in flight. Modern flying helmets have a system known as Head-Up Visual Display, in which digital flight information is screened onto the inside of the pilot's visor.

THE GROWTH OF THE AIR FORCE

In 1914, Europe was plunged into World War I, a war that raged across the continent and in which it soon became clear that aircraft could make a significant contribution. Although the United States did not join the war for another three years, the government realized that it lagged behind the European powers, having few aircraft and scant resources. Even before war broke out, Congress established the Aviation Section of the Signal Corps on July 18, 1914. Nonetheless, this was weak when compared to the air forces of the warring nations, all of which had large units of combat aircraft. And when the United States entered the war in 1917, the government faced criticism about the lack of air power.

In response, President Woodrow Wilson formed the Army Air Service on May 24, 1918, and invested in its strength and technology. Many U.S. pilots had already gained air combat experience by flying with other Allied air forces or as part of the American Expeditionary Forces (AEF), which was established in 1917 and fought in the final year of World War I. Captain Edward V. Rickenbacker, for instance, became a true fighter ace, personally shooting down 26 enemy aircraft. Taking advantage of such experience, President Wilson passed legislation that brought the Army Air Service to a strength of nearly 200,000 men and 11,754 aircraft by November 1918. However, November 1918 was also the month in which the war ended, and the Army Air Service was dramatically cut back.

While the European nations involved in World War I had created separate air forces, the U.S. Air Service remained as part of the Army. On July 2, 1926, the Air Corps Act redesignated the Air

Captain Eddie Rickenbacker was one of the great U.S. fighter aces of World War I. Formerly a successful race-car driver, Rickenbacker joined the 94th Aero Squadron in France in 1917. By the end of the war, he had shot down 26 enemy aircraft.

Service as the Army Air Corps, and in 1935, all Air Corps units fell under the command of General Headquarters Air Force.

As with the Army and Navy, it was World War II (1939–1945) that revolutionized the Air Force. At the outbreak of war, the Army Air Corps had 24,000 personnel and 1,500 combat aircraft, still far below the strength of the European air forces. Realizing this, the U.S. government embarked on a massive program of expanding its air units. On June 20, 1941, six months before the United States actually entered the war, the Air Corps was renamed the United States Army Air Force (USAAF).

During World War II, the USAAF grew to an immense size, peaking in 1944 at around 60,000 combat aircraft, 20,000 support aircraft, and 2,372,292 personnel. U.S. industry also turned out some of the best aircraft of the entire war. Aircraft such as the P-51 Mustang long-range fighter and the B-17 Flying Fortress bomber were vital in bringing enemy air forces and industry to their knees. By mid-1944, U.S. and Allied air forces had complete air superiority over both Germany and Japan. Indeed, it was U.S. air power that finally brought World War II to an end, when the USAAF B-29 Superfortresses dropped atomic bombs over Hiroshima and Nagasaki in 1945.

AN INDEPENDENT AIR FORCE

World War II proved the value of U.S. air power. Although many units were disbanded as the conflict ended, the government recognized that the USAAF should have a new status. On September 18, 1947, the U.S. Air Force (USAF) was officially formed as a separate command and given equality with the Army and the Navy. General Carl A. Spaatz was the first USAF chief of staff.

As the world war ended, the **Cold War** began. After 1949, the year in which the Soviet Union tested its first atomic bomb, one of the main roles of the USAF was to defend against or deploy nuclear weapons. The Strategic Air Command (SAC) was created in 1946. Its mission was to launch nuclear-capable bombers against the Soviet Union in the event of a nuclear war. To perform this role, the

This bomber crewman is from the USAAF 8th Army Air Force stationed in England in 1945. USAAF bomber crews flew thousands of dangerous daylight missions attacking the heartland of German industrial power in massive B-17 Flying Fortress heavy bombers.

USAF created new long-range bombers, including the B-36 Peacemaker and, later, the enormous B-52 Stratofortress. In the 1960s, SAC also took over control of many of the United States' intercontinental ballistic missiles (ICBMs), designed to be launched from silos on the U.S. mainland.

Nuclear-weapons deployment was only one aspect of the new Air Force. By 1950, it was back in conventional air-combat roles with the onset of the Korean War (1950–1953). In Korea, jet aircraft clashed for the first time in combat, the USAF represented by the North American F-86 Sabre and North Korea by MiG 15 jets. The battle was close-fought—750 U.S. aircraft were destroyed in the war for over 950 North

The Boeing B-29 Superfortress "Enola Gay"—the most famous aircraft in history—lands in the Marianas Islands, the Pacific, 1945. On August 6, 1945, "Enola Gay" dropped the atomic bomb on the Japanese city of Hiroshima.

Korean and Chinese jets. The 1950s was also a time in which the USAF steadily made the shift from turboprop aircraft to faster and more powerful jet aircraft, supersonic flight having already been achieved—on October 14, 1947, test pilot Chuck Yeager flew his Bell XS-1 faster than the speed of sound. It is worth noting, however, that turboprops retain many transportation and surveillance roles in the Air Force even today.

In the early 1960s, the USAF became involved in another conflict in the Far East, this time in the troubled country of Vietnam. The United States was steadily dragged into the war between North and South Vietnam, and for over 10 years, the Air Force flew thousands of combat and supply missions.

The Vietnam War (1963–1975) was one of the greatest periods of technological development in the Air Force. Helicopters were the principle method of transporting troops and supplies, and combat helicopters armed with rockets and machine guns were developed. In the face of such lethal air defenses, classic aircraft, such as the McDonnell Douglas F-4 Phantom and Republic F-105 Thunderchief, conducted missions over North Vietnam. Precision-guided bombs and air-to-air missiles (AAMs) were used for the first time, with impressive results. The Air Force also conducted some of the heaviest aerial bombardments in history at this time. During Operation Rolling Thunder (1965–1968), for instance, USAF, U.S. Navy, and U.S. Marine Corps aircraft dropped over one million tons of bombs over North Vietnam.

The Vietnam War was ultimately a defeat for the United States. The Air Force, however, had shown that it could achieve complete air superiority and was a powerful force for waging war. Following the Vietnam conflict, the USAF continued with what has proved to be an inexorable rise to technological dominance.

In the 1970s and 1980s, new aircraft emerged, such as the F-15 Eagle, the F-16 Fighting Falcon, the A-10 Thunderbolt, and the E-3 Sentry. These aircraft brought new standards to military aviation with lethal advanced weapons, such as laser-guided bombs and the A-10's enormous tank-busting GAU-8 multibarreled cannon, which is capable of firing 75 high-explosive armor-piercing shells every second. The Air Force also acquired a large fleet of airborne-refueling aircraft and long-range supply aircraft, giving it the ability to fuel and resupply without touching down.

Two Boeing B-52 Stratofortresses conduct a high-altitude bombing raid over North Vietnam in 1966. Each bomber could carry a massive 69,996 lb (31,750 kg) of bombs. The Stratofortress was recently used against enemy positions in Afghanistan.

THE MODERN AIR FORCE

For much of the Cold War, the U.S. and Soviet air forces had similar capabilities and strengths. However, during the 1980s, the United States' great industrial wealth let it leap ahead in technology, quality of personnel, and tactical training. A landmark was the emergence of the revolutionary F-117A "stealth" fighter, a jet that looks like something out of a science-fiction movie and that is capable of flying through enemy airspace without being detected by enemy radar. In 1992, the B-2 stealth bomber also emerged.

BRIGADIER GENERAL WILLIAM MITCHELL

One of the most significant figures in the history of the USAF is General William "Billy" Mitchell. He began a military career in the Army during the Spanish-American War of 1889. In 1915, he joined the aviation section of the Signal Corps, and learned to fly in 1916. During World War I, Mitchell was an innovative and daring air commander in France. He was the first American airman to fly across enemy lines, and he launched the world's first major bombing attack, using 1,500 aircraft.

After the war, he gave the first demonstration of dropping combat troops by parachute. He also became assistant chief of the Air Service and argued vehemently for the creation of a separate air force. He retired on February 1, 1926, still arguing—and warning—that Japan's aircraft carriers were a threat to the U.S. fleet at Hawaii. Mitchell died on February 19, 1936; five years later, Pearl Harbor was attacked. Military officials suddenly recognized how visionary Mitchell had been, and many of his ideas were now implemented. In 1948, General Carl Spaatz, chief of staff of the newly created U.S. Air Force, presented Mitchell's son with a medal authorized by Congress that honored his father's contribution to U.S. military aviation.

The 1980s saw the Air Force engage in many operations, including Grenada (1983), Libya (1986), and Panama (1989). Even after the end of the Cold War in 1989, when the Berlin Wall was finally pulled down, a year rarely went by without the Air Force

The General Dynamics F-111 first entered service with the USAF in 1964 but was decommissioned in 1995. F-111s were involved in the bombing of Libya in 1986, and served with devastating effect in the Gulf War of 1990–91.

being sent into action somewhere in the world.

In the Gulf War (1990–1991), USAF aircraft devastated Iraqi military forces and communications. Such was the efficiency of their bombardments that the land campaign to expel Iraqi forces from Kuwait lasted only 100 hours and cost few lives. USAF units operate in the Middle East to this day, but the Air Force has performed hundreds of other missions around the world since the end of the Gulf War, particularly in Europe, in the former country of Yugoslavia, between 1993 and 1999.

Today, the USAF is engaged in the war against terrorism,

pounding enemy strongholds in the mountains of Afghanistan in support of ground-troop operations. The firepower, surveillance, and reach of the Air Force has attained such levels that no professional army in the world can stand up to its force in an open campaign. The war on terrorism is a difficult one for the U.S. military, but the Air Force is, as always, playing a major part in protecting the nation.

A pilot aboard a USAF B-52H Stratofortress maintains a vigilant watch during strikes against the Federal Republic of Yugoslavia, 1999. The B-52 can remain airborne for over 35 hours.

STRUCTURE AND COMMANDS

The Air Force has undergone many changes over the last 10 years. Its command structure enables it to respond to crises in a matter of hours. Just like the poster appearing on the walls of many USAF bases says, "The mission of the United States Air Force is to fly and fight, and don't you ever forget it."

Although the Air Force has many other roles, this statement is still accurate. Since it was created in 1947, the USAF has been in the frontline of most U.S. combat missions around the world.

THE ORGANIZATION OF THE USAF

Like the other branches of the U.S. armed forces, the USAF is ultimately commanded by the President and the Secretary of Defense. Just below this level of authority is the Commander-in-Chief (CINC) of the USAF, who sits on the Joint Chiefs of Staff (JCS).

The Commander-in-Chief is ultimately responsible for Air Force deployments and operations. In a time of war, however, control of the USAF passes over to what is known as a Unified Command. A Unified Command contains elements of the Army, Navy, and Air Force and exercises responsibility for a particular geographical region of the world.

Left: A C-5A Galaxy heavy-cargo transport aircraft unloads a light tank through its hinged nose section. Each aircraft can lift a maximum combat payload of 291,000 lbs (130,950 kg).

The Air Force itself is split into a number of commands—huge units that each run different areas of USAF operations. Currently, there are nine major commands.

Air Combat Command (ACC)

The ACC is one of the largest and most important of the commands. It operates all of the USAF's warplanes—more than 1,700 combat aircraft. It has responsibility not only for fighter and bomber aircraft, but also for the deployment of air-launched nuclear weapons in the case of a nuclear conflict. ACC is based at Langley Air Force Base (AFB), Virginia.

AIR FORCE UNITS

The structure of USAF units is complex and can be confusing, so here is a basic guide to their structure:

Flight—the smallest unit, consisting of around four aircraft and led by flight leader, usually a captain.

Squadron—a squadron consists of several flights, usually four. Around eight large transport planes or 24 fighter jets will make up a squadron, and it is led by a lieutenant-colonel or a major.

Group—the group is made up of several squadrons. The number of squadrons and aircraft involved varies greatly, depending on the requirement and the resources available.

Wing—like the group, a wing consists of several squadrons and is usually commanded by a "Wing Commander."

An F-117 Night Hawk "stealth" fighter refuels in midair from a Boeing KC-135 Stratotanker. USAF Air Mobility Command operates a fleet of over 546 Stratotankers, each aircraft costing $40 million.

Air Mobility Command (AMC)

AMC's role is the rapid deployment of U.S. armed forces units around the world in support of operations, a job it does using fleets of long-range transport aircraft. It is based at Scott AFB, Illinois.

Air Force Materiel Command (AFMC)

The AFMC was created on July 1, 1992. It is responsible for developing and maintaining USAF aircraft and technology, and giving the USAF the best tools of war. AFMC tests and evaluates new aircraft and weapons, and employs around 90,000 personnel. Its headquarters are at Wright-Patterson AFB, Ohio.

A McDonnell Douglas Delta II rocket blasts off on the journey to space to deliver a satellite into low-earth orbit. The Delta II stands at 126 ft (41 m) tall and is primarily used to deploy Navstar Global Positioning System (GPS) navigational satellites.

Air Force Space Command (AFSC)

AFSC was created on September 1, 1982, and is headquartered at Peterson AFB, Colorado. With more than 40,000 personnel, the AFSC maintains and, if necessary, deploys USAF ICBMs, controlling approximately one-third of the United States' entire nuclear capability. The AFSC also launches military satellites, conducts space-based surveillance, and provides navigational facilities to military units on the ground.

Air Force Special Operations Command (AFSOC)

AFSOC specializes in **covert** or high-risk operations. Its main role is the stealthy **infiltration** of U.S. special forces soldiers using airborne means, but it will also deploy weapons when necessary. AFSOC has 12,000 personnel and around 100 aircraft, both fixed and rotary-wing (rotary-wing aircraft are also known as helicopters).

Three USAF aircraft make a sweep over the former Yugoslavia as part of Operation Deny Flight. The aircraft are (from left to right): an A-10 Thunderbolt, an FA-18 Hornet, and the F-16 Fighting Falcon.

Pacific Air Forces (PACAF)

PACAF is a geographical command responsible for 100 million square miles (258 sq km) of territory between the west coast of the United States and the east coast of Africa. With more than 45,000 personnel and over 300 warplanes, PACAF can respond to crisis or conflict in any of the 44 countries in its region. It has its headquarters at Hickham AFB, Hawaii.

Here, a USAF B-1B Lancer bomber takes off from the Diego Garcia Airbase in the Indian Ocean on a strike mission against Al Qaeda training camps in Afghanistan, October 2001. As a part of Operation Enduring Freedom, the carefully targeted attacks helped bring down the Taliban regime and undermine Al Qaeda terrorist operations.

An F-16 Fighting Falcon launches an air-to-air missile. Although the F-16 is a fighter, during Operation Allied Force in the former Yugoslavia in 1999, they also destroyed enemy tanks, radar sites, and buildings.

Air Education and Training Command (AETC)

AETC's job is to train future airmen and other personnel for service in the USAF. It uses 1,600 aircraft, 1,400 recruiters, and 28 squadrons to accomplish this task. Around 36,000 people each year complete the USAF basic training course at Lackland AFB, Texas.

United States Air Forces in Europe (USAFE)

The USAFE has its headquarters at Ramstein Air Base, Germany. Using around 225 military aircraft and 35,000 personnel, USAFE conducts USAF operations in Europe and Africa and also supports European **NATO** air forces when required. The USAFE has seen a lot of action over the last 15 years, using more than 180 aircraft in the Gulf War and flying many humanitarian and combat operations in Africa and southern Europe.

Air Force Reserve Command (AFRC)

AFRC is the newest of the major USAF commands. It was created on February 17, 1997, and has the role of providing additional power to USAF missions when necessary. AFRC has 447 military aircraft, 99 percent of which can be brought into action within 72 hours. AFRC also contains many support units, such as medical, engineering, communications, and transportation teams.

AIR FORCE ROLES

The obvious duty of the USAF is fighting wars, but there are many different roles within this category. There are three main types of combat aircraft, each with a specific job.

AIR NATIONAL GUARD

The Air National Guard (ANG) is the defender of United States' airspace. Like the Army's National Guard, the ANG has a responsibility for federal and state defense, but it also provides 100 percent of the United States' air-defense interceptor force and about 50 percent of the USAF's support duties. It is manned full-time by civilian personnel, who have a military status within the ANG. In total, it has over 106,000 personnel and 88 flying units regularly deployed overseas. ANG aircraft flew combat missions in the Gulf War, and since then have been regularly used in humanitarian and **contingency operations**. One of their most important current roles is protecting the U.S. skies from further terrorist attacks as part of Operation Noble Eagle.

Fighter aircraft, such as F-15 Eagle, F-16 Fighting Falcon, and YF-22 Rapier jets, are used to defend U.S. troops and citizens against enemy aircraft. USAF fighters are made to be fast, maneuverable, tough, and destructive, and they are mainly armed with air-to-air missiles (AAMs), such as the AIM-9 Sidewinder or the AIM-120 AMRAAM. The role of strike/attack aircraft is to attack enemy ground targets, often in advance of an assault by ground forces. During the Gulf War, for example, U.S. F-111, F-117, and F-15E jets destroyed thousands of Iraqi military vehicles and almost all Iraqi communications and radar systems.

The Air Force also uses strategic bombers. These are huge aircraft, such as the B-52 Stratofortress and Rockwell B-1B, and their role is primarily to produce massive bombardments of enemy ground positions or to launch nuclear missiles from the air. Strategic bombers tend to be used only in situations in which there is little or no risk from enemy ground fire, because they are slow aircraft and difficult to maneuver.

Combat, however, is only one aspect of USAF duties. Another vital mission is airborne reconnaissance. Aircraft such as the E-3 AWACS, E-8 Joint Stars, the RC-135V, and the Lockheed U-2R can provide detailed surveillance images of the ground below them from a high altitude, regardless of the weather or battlefield conditions. These images are transmitted to Army, Navy, or Air Force units for tactical use. Surveillance aircraft also perform combat flight-control services, warning USAF aircraft of enemy planes and directing them into the right position to attack.

A similar, but more aggressive, role of USAF aircraft is called "combat support." Combat support involves aircraft deliberately destroying or jamming enemy communications, radar, or SAM (surface-to-air missile) systems.

The type of aircraft used in this role includes the General Dynamics/Grumman EF-111A and the McDonnell Douglas F-4G "Wild Weasel" (both now out of service), and the EC-130 Hercules. By jamming or destroying enemy systems, the combat-support aircraft provide fighters, attack aircraft, and strategic bombers with safer air corridors and greater chances of successfully completing their missions.

Many USAF aircraft are not involved directly in combat, but are still vital to effective air operations. Boeing KC-135 Stratotankers provide in-flight refueling for other U.S. aircraft, giving them the ability to fly to international locations without having to land and refuel. Every year, USAF transport aircraft carry millions of tons of equipment around the world. The real value of military transport aircraft is their speed. Whereas a ship can take up to a week to sail from the United States to the Middle East, transport aircraft, such as the C-5 Galaxy and C-141 Starlifter, can do it in a day, and deliver anything from tanks to troops.

Apart from the roles outlined, USAF aircraft perform a multitude of other duties, including deploying special forces units, flying prominent or important people, training airmen, and even displaying flying techniques at air shows. Each role contributes to making the Air Force capable of tackling any military, peacemaking, or humanitarian mission anywhere in the world.

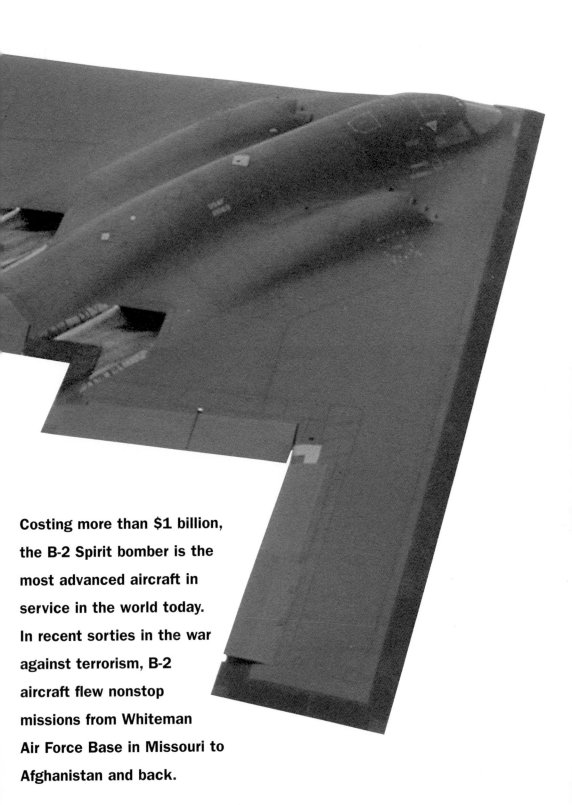

Costing more than $1 billion, the B-2 Spirit bomber is the most advanced aircraft in service in the world today. In recent sorties in the war against terrorism, B-2 aircraft flew nonstop missions from Whiteman Air Force Base in Missouri to Afghanistan and back.

TRAINING FOR COMBAT: U.S. AIR FORCE PILOT TRAINING

It takes well over a year to create a USAF pilot. Many of those who start the training are not there to complete the program at the end of it, but those who do remain, stand apart as the elite. Pilot training is one of the most demanding programs of military instruction in the world, and only those with strong bodies and exceptional minds make the grade.

It should be remembered that there are literally hundreds of different careers in the Air Force. Engineers, cooks, radar operators, lawyers, technicians, designers, administrators—the list of different jobs runs on and on. However, the fact remains that the public is initially most interested in what it takes to become a USAF pilot, as this chapter will explain.

MILITARY BOOT CAMP

What pilots and all other Air Force personnel have in common is that they have to undergo the six-week Air Force Basic Training (BT) program held at the 737th Air Force Base, in San Antonio, Texas. More than 35,000 new recruits pass through this program

Left: A USAF pilot checks over his right wing before takeoff in his F-16 Fighting Falcon jet. It usually takes just over a year to train a USAF pilot once he or she has completed the six-week basic training program.

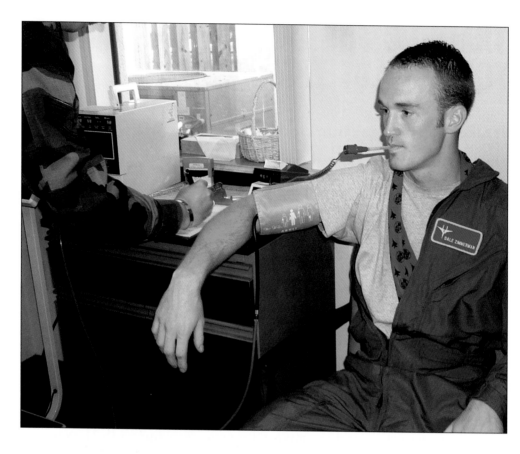

This trainee pilot is given a physical examination by a USAF doctor at Tyndale Air Force Base, Florida, prior to taking an orientation flight in an F-15 Eagle, August 2000. All pilots have to undergo rigorous physical and mental tests in order to show that they will be tough enough to withstand combat conditions.

every year. Although a small proportion of these people will go on to become pilots, the six weeks of BT make no distinction between individuals of whatever rank or role.

The first week of BT is mostly spent sorting out administration and processing matters. New recruits are met at San Antonio Airport by their Training Instructors (TIs), who then take them on a

BEING A FIGHTER PILOT

Major Fritz Heck, USAF fighter pilot, recalls how he became a pilot and what life is like in the USAF:

"I got a brochure in the mail when I was a junior at high school for the Air Force Academy. I had always wanted to fly airplanes ever since I was a little kid. I looked at the brochure and thought this looked like a good way to get to where I wanted to be. So, I mailed the application to the Air Force Academy and sent the application to my congressman for review. I then had to have an interview with my congressman, and I was one of the few to get a nomination. Then my dream came true—I was accepted into the Air Force Academy.

"I flew combat operations in Operation Northern Watch, Operation Southern Watch, Joint Guard, Deny Flight, Provide Comfort, and Allied Force. It was a very busy time for me, and a combat operation was one of the most exciting things I ever did. Now, I'm a test pilot. Planes come into our base for servicing and maintenance. It's up to me test them out and really push them to their limits to make sure that they're suitable for flying in combat."

A USAF pilot makes a final navigation check before a combat operation over the former Yugoslavia in 1999.

bus to Lackland AFB. The first week involves new recruits being assigned a dormitory, receiving their uniform, having a close haircut, learning basic rules and regulations, and filling in forms. Those who are unfit or overweight are sometimes put on the PT Flight, a program of intense physical exercise to bring them into shape. The recruits receive vaccinations and a dental inspection to make sure that they are fit to train.

Actual Air Force BT begins the second week. Although the Air Force BT does not have the tough reputation of Marine Corps or Army Rangers training, the initial weeks are surprisingly similar and demanding. The TIs are hard and critical individuals, who spot every mistake and pounce on every sign of inefficiency. The recruits do increasingly tougher physical exercises under the watchful gaze of the TI, and they also learn the basics of saluting, parade-ground drill (known as flight drill), and how to clean and prepare their dormitory for inspection.

On average, they will receive two dormitory inspections per week, and are harshly punished for any failings. Academic classes also begin. During BT, recruits can expect to do 40 hours of class-room work. Subjects covered include Air Force history, Air Force organization, financial management, customs and courtesies, health and fitness, and human relations (discussing how to work as a team). The TIs expect to see the recruits work as hard in the class-room as they do in the exercise yard.

In weeks three and four, the recruits are tested on everything they have learned to date. To keep their feet on the ground, they will also be put on "Kitchen Patrol," which means helping to keep the camp

The T-37 Tweet is one of the USAF's principal training aircraft for recruit pilots. It is inexpensive—each aircraft costs just over $164,000—and has a top speed of around 360 mph (579 km/h). The pilot and instructor sit side by side in the cockpit.

kitchens spotlessly clean. Physical training gets harder and harder, but the recruits also acquire basic principles of military operations. Week five is called "Warrior Week," and for good reason. For the entire week, the recruits live out in the field in tents, learning survival skills, shooting the M16 rifle, and tackling tough military obstacle courses.

They also experience chemical-warfare training. Part of this involves a spell in the "gas chamber," a CS-gas-filled room in which the recruit must take off his gas mask twice and recount his name,

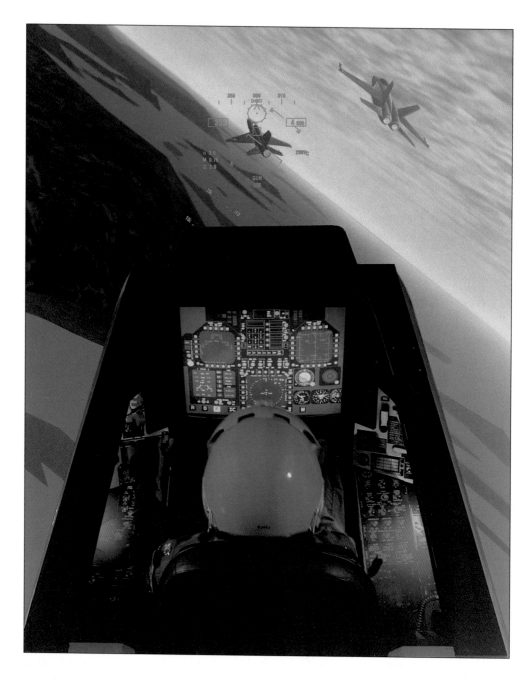

This trainee pilot is "flying" the Modular Aircrew Simulation System (MASS). Made by McDonnell Douglas Training Systems, MASS is a portable simulator that can be configured to a number of different aircraft interiors, including the F-15 Eagle and FA-18 Hornet.

rank, and social security number. The TIs also give the recruits mental tests and exercises that push their ability to work as a team and show initiative.

After Warrior Week, the final week is spent winding down. Unless the recruits make any serious mistakes in this last week, they will pass through the next level of training. A recruit intent on being a pilot then faces over a year of additional training.

PILOT TRAINING

Flight training takes place at Randolph AFB, Texas. There are three main stages. First, the pilot candidates undergo Introductory Flight Training (IFT), in which they receive 50 hours of flying instruction to gain their private pilot license (although many pilot candidates arrive in Randolph having already acquired this license).

After IFT, recruits go in one of two directions. They can attend either the Euro-NATO Joint Jet Pilot Training (ENJJPT) or the Joint Specialized Undergraduate Pilot Training (JSUPT). Both courses are extremely demanding and last around 52–54 weeks. ENJJPT teaches the pilot candidate to fly military jets in association with NATO allies, and some instruction is carried out by European officers. By contrast, JSUPT focuses on USAF flying and aircraft. This book will examine in more detail the processes of JSUPT.

JSUPT usually lasts 52 weeks. At the end, candidates will be fully qualified pilots. There are three phases to training. Phase one lasts for one month and consists mainly of classroom instruction in the basics of military aviation. Academic work is extremely important and highly technical in USAF pilot training. Courses include aerospace physiology, fundamentals of flying, aerodynamics, mission planning, navigation, aviation weather, crisis handling, military intelligence, and theoretical training in the aircraft they will fly. All academic work is tested at regular intervals, and the pilot candidates must pass each test to complete the course.

Phase two sees the pilot candidates begin their military flying training. This phase lasts for six months and is normally conducted in T-34, T-37, or T-6 Texan II training aircraft. Phase two teaches the pilot candidates the fundamentals of flying military aircraft. They will spend time in the air and also in flying simulators on the ground, and the instructors will test their ability to respond to in-flight crises and problems. In particular, instructors will look to see that candidates can cope with stressful events while suffering from the extreme physical effects of flying a modern jet.

If the pilot candidates pass all stages of phase two, they will then proceed to one of four advanced training tracks, depending on what type of aircraft they want to fly. These tracks are as follows, alongside the length of training, the training aircraft used, and the training bases:

• Advanced Fighter: six months; USAF T-38 aircraft; Columbus AFB, Vance AFB, Laughlin AFB
• Advanced Tanker/Transport/Bomber: six months; USAF T-1 aircraft; Columbus AFB, Vance AFB, Laughlin AFB
• Advanced Prop: six months; USN T-44; NAS Corpus Christi
• Advanced Helicopter (Army): seven months; various aircraft; Fort Rucker

An AIM 120 Advanced Medium-Range Air-to-Air Missile (AMRAAM) is inspected before loading onto an F-16 Fighting Falcon. Trainee pilots usually do not have the opportunity to fire or drop live munitions during their initial program of flight training.

The third phase, advanced training, is the most demanding stage for the pilot candidates. They will be tested constantly under high-pressure situations, and both mind and body will be pushed to the very limits of endurance. If they can make it through, however, they will successfully graduate as USAF pilots.

Ironically, this training may be only the beginning. Once they are trained in a particular style of aviation, they must go on to a distinct

TRAINING FOR THE PRESSURES OF FLYING

During their pilot training, pilot candidates spend time with the Aerospace Physiology (AP) section. The AP section tests the pilot candidates' ability to cope with the physical strain of flying modern aircraft. One test involves a piece of equipment called the hypobaric altitude chamber. This is a chamber on the ground capable of simulating the low air pressures and reduced oxygen levels a pilot would feel at high altitude if the plane suddenly depressurized.

The pilot candidates sit wearing oxygen masks in the chamber while the pressure is lowered to the equivalent of 50,000 ft (16,400 m) altitude. Then they are told to remove the masks. As soon as they do so, they start to suffer from the effects of oxygen deprivation to the brain. They feel light-headed, dizzy, nauseous, and find it hard to think straight. For a short period of time, the instructors will try to get them to accomplish mental tasks to see how they cope with the problem. However, they are soon told to put their masks back on—they will lose consciousness if they do not. Other tests in the AP section include parachute and ejection-seat training, and also subjecting the pilots to high **G-forces** to see how well they cope.

squadron and train in an individual aircraft, such as the F-15 Eagle or F-16 Falcon (for fighter pilots) or the C-130 Hercules (for transportation pilots).

The length of training ensures that those who become USAF

pilots are among the elite. Today, no nation on earth trains its pilots better than the United States. Indeed, in recent examples of aerial combat, the USAF has almost always come out on top.

Trainee aircrew receive instruction in a C-130 Hercules flight simulator at Little Rock Air Force Base, Arizona. Simulators allow aircrew to train for in-flight disasters in total safety. The simulator stands on hydraulic pistons that realistically imitate the actual movements of the aircraft.

AIRCRAFT AND TECHNOLOGY OF THE U.S. AIR FORCE

The U.S. Air Force has set the world standard for technical excellence in military aviation. Its aircraft possess the ultimate in firepower, speed, and computer technology.

In World War II, a U.S. fighter pilot flying into combat in a P-51 Mustang, for example, had a maximum speed of 437 mph (784 km/h). This speed meant that, if he spotted enemy aircraft in the far distance, he only had a couple of minutes in which to prepare for action. His aircraft was armed with six 0.5-inch machine guns, and could also carry two 1,000-lb (454-kg) bombs or six 5-inch rockets. At full power, using his Packard Rolls-Royce Merlin V-12 piston engine, he could climb to 30,000 ft (9,145 m) in 13 minutes. Fitted with external fuel tanks, the Mustang had a maximum flying range of 2,080 miles (3,347 km), and it could operate to a maximum height of 41,900 ft (12,770 m). The Mustang was one of the greatest fighter aircraft of the entire war, and few enemy aircraft could match its capabilities.

Now, leap forward 50 years and see how the experience of modern USAF fighter pilots differs from that of their predecessors.

Left: The EA-6B Prowler is central to the USAF's electronic-warfare operations. It contains the ALQ-99 tactical jammer for jamming enemy communications, and antiradiation missiles for destroying enemy radar.

In this instance, the pilot is flying a McDonnell Douglas F-15 Eagle, possibly the best all-around fighter aircraft in the world today.

Seeing the enemy in the far distance, the F-15 pilot has only two or three seconds in which to make evasive or combat maneuvers— the Eagle's maximum speed is over 1,650 mph (2,655 km/h). Its two Pratt & Whitney F100-P220 jet engines each produce 14,370 lb (6,518 kg) of thrust, letting it climb at a dizzying 50,000 ft (15,240 m) per minute. The F-15's range can extend to 3,450 miles (5,560 km), and in addition, the aircraft has a practical altitude ceiling of 60,000 ft (18,290 m).

Perhaps the most striking difference between the Mustang and the Eagle lies in armaments. The Eagle is armed with a 20-mm M16A-1 cannon, eight guided air-to-air missiles, and more than 16,000 lb (7,258 kg) of bombs and other missile technologies. Its destructive force is astounding. Using an AIM-120 Advance Medium-Range Air-to-Air Missile (AMRAAM), for example, the Eagle is able to engage and destroy an enemy aircraft over 20 miles (32 km) away, well beyond the visual range of the pilot. Laser-guided bombs, such as the GBU-24 Paveway III, can explode a 2000-lb (907-kg) warhead on target with an accuracy of only a few feet from the aiming point.

Most dramatically, an Eagle can also drop a B61 tactical nuclear bomb, which has an explosive force equivalent to 500,000 tons of dynamite. These weapons are only a selection of those the Eagle can carry, and few who have ever been attacked by such an aircraft can forget the experience, if they survive. This comparison between the Mustang and the Eagle shows how far the USAF has come in only

An F-15A Eagle releases an AIM-7 Sparrow air-to-air missile. In the Gulf War, 22 Iraqi fixed-wing aircraft and three Iraqi helicopters were shot down using Sparrow missiles. Once fired, they are guided to the target by an internal radar system and are very hard to escape.

half a century. Today's pilots face the same life-or-death challenges the pilots in World War II faced, but their war machines are infinitely more advanced.

The Eagle is only one of the USAF's fleet of superior aircraft. This chapter will look at the different aircraft that fulfill the USAF's fighter and ground-attack roles. Each of these aircraft types represent the best in their class, and they demonstrate why the USAF is the world's dominant air force.

FIGHTERS

Fighters engage and destroy enemy aircraft in air-to-air combat. Actually, few USAF aircraft are totally dedicated to the fighter role. Most fighter-capable aircraft are designated as "strike fighters," meaning that they perform ground-attack duties as well as air interceptions. However, within the United States itself, the Air National Guard deploys McDonnell Douglas F-15 Eagles and General Dynamics F-16 Fighting Falcons dedicated to domestic air-interception duties. F-15 units are based on the west and east coasts of the United States and on Hawaii to protect from overseas attacks.

The F-16 Fighting Falcon is the most maneuverable fighter aircraft in the world. Even with a full load, the F-16 can make maneuvers that inflict a force of nine times the strength of gravity on the pilot and airframe. This force is at the outer limits of human endurance.

ULTIMATE EXPLOSIVES

During the war in Afghanistan in 2002, a fearful weapon was dropped on enemy positions that caught the attention of the world. This was the BLU-82 15,000-lb (6,804 kg) bomb. The BLU-82 was originally developed to create instant landing zones for helicopters in the jungles of Vietnam. It consists of a huge metal case filled with 12,600 lb (5,715 kg) of jellied explosive. The bomb is so big that it has to be mounted on a cargo palette and pushed out the back of an MC-130 transport aircraft. When it hits the ground, the explosion is so big that everything within a diameter of 1,829 ft (600 m) is vaporized. In the Gulf War, 11 such bombs were dropped, mainly to cause psychological damage on the enemy. In Afghanistan, the BLU-82 was used as an "earthquake" bomb to kill Taliban fighters hiding in mountainous cave systems.

F-16 units are found across the U.S. landmass, providing internal air defense. Whether serving in the Air National Guard or in the regular Air Force overseas, these two fighters present a formidable barrier to any enemy's attempt to control airspace.

The F-16 was developed in the 1970s as a highly maneuverable air-superiority fighter. It can fly at 1,350 mph (2,172 km/h) and is armed with one 20-mm M61 cannon, AMRAAM, Sparrow and Sidewinder AAMs, and a weapons load of 17,200 lb (7,802 kg). This craft is unusual in that the F-16 pilot does not fly using a central joystick. Instead, the control is a small handle only a few inches high set to the right-hand side of the pilot's seat.

Interestingly, the F-16 is the most commercially successful warplane since World War II. More than 4,000 have been produced, and it is used by over 18 different nations.

Yet the days of the F-15 and F-16 in the USAF are slowly coming to an end. Two new fighters are replacing them as part of the USAF's Advanced Tactical Fighter program. One is the Lockheed F-22 Rapier, a highly maneuverable, ultra high-tech fighter, which has sophisticated features, such as thrust vectoring (the direction of blast from the jets can be altered to increase maneuverability) and radar-absorbent materials to diminish its appearance on enemy radar. The other is the Lockheed Martin X-35 Joint Strike Fighter (JSF). This aircraft, a joint project between the United States and Canada, is still in its development stage, but it promises to be a superb fighter with Short Takeoff and Landing (STL) ability—the jet exhausts can be angled to let the jet take off from, or land on, short landing strips. Although the F-15 and F-16 will serve for many years to come as fine aircraft, the Rapier and JSF will keep the USAF at the top of aviation technology.

STRIKE FIGHTERS AND ATTACK AIRCRAFT

Wherever it is deployed, the USAF has total air superiority. Consequently, few enemy forces will actually fight the USAF in the air. Those that have recently been tempted to do so, such as Iraq in the Gulf War, were utterly decimated. With few air-to-air combat duties, the USAF is usually employed in attacking ground targets.

Two types of aircraft fulfill this role. One is the "strike fighter," a versatile fighter aircraft that is also capable of making ground-attack missions. The other is the attack aircraft, these being airplanes dedi-cated to pounding enemy land targets.

The USAF has a vast range of strike/attack aircraft. One of its most important is actually a variant of the F-15 Eagle, known as the F-15E. The F-15E has the same performance abilities as the stan-dard fighter version, but carries more advanced electronics and is also able to support heavier weights of ammunition, bombs, and missiles. F-15Es have been used hard over recent years, bombing targets from the deserts of Iraq to the snow-covered mountains of

A USAF engineer loads an AIM-9 Sidewinder missile onto an F-16 Fighting Falcon prior to takeoff. Besides the Sidewinder, the main air-to-air missiles of the USAF are currently the AIM-7 Sparrow and the AIM-120A AMRAAM.

The F-117 Night Hawk's first combat operations were conducted in the Gulf War, when they made direct hits on over 1,600 important military and political targets. The Night Hawk holds the record for the longest mission conducted by a single-seat fighter—18.5 hours.

Afghanistan, and they have always proved themselves to be excellent strike aircraft. By far, however, the most technologically advanced strike fighter is the F-117 Night Hawk, the "Stealth Fighter." The

Night Hawk employs what is known as "low observables" technology, also known as "stealth" technology. A special radar-absorbent material is applied to the surface of the aircraft. This material, combined with the slim angular shape of the Night Hawk, absorbs and deflects enemy radar signals and makes it almost invisible to enemy electronic surveillance. The aircraft also uses special

An A-10 Thunderbolt of the 81st Tactical Fighter Wing makes a maneuver. The Thunderbolt was designed to operate in close support of ground troops at low levels. Its titanium armor enables it to survive direct hits from heavy-caliber and armor-piercing bullets.

engines that produce little noise, no visible exhaust, and little heat signature. All these capabilities enable the Night Hawk to creep up on enemy targets, cruising at a speed of around 580 mph (933 km/h) before delivering up to 4,000 lb (1,814 kg) of precision-guided high-explosive bombs. During Operation Desert Storm, F-117 aircraft flew 1,271 combat **sorties** in 42 days without a single loss—testimony to the superiority of the Night Hawk.

Not all the USAF's strike aircraft are as sophisticated as the F-117, each of which costs $45 million. Another veteran of the Gulf War is the Fairchild A-10 Thunderbolt II, each costing a much more reasonable $9.8 million. The Thunderbolt is a tank-busting aircraft. It is slow—maximum speed is about 439 mph (706 km/h)—but it is heavily protected with titanium armor and can carry up to 16,000 lb (7,258 kg) of bombs and AGM-65 Maverick air-to-surface missiles (ASMs). However, its main weapon is the enormous General Electric GAU-8/A Avenger 30-mm seven-barrel cannon. This lethal weapon fires armor-piercing **depleted-uranium** ammunition at either 2,100 or 4,200 rounds per minute. Just a two-second burst from this mighty weapon will destroy the largest main battle tanks. In the Gulf War, Thunderbolts destroyed hundreds of Iraqi vehicles and became one of the USAF's most feared ground-attack weapons.

The USAF's huge inventory of weapons includes many more than the ones listed in this section. Air-launched Tomahawk **cruise missiles** can fly hundreds of miles, hugging the terrain, before hitting a target with pinpoint precision. A Boeing B-52 Strato-fortress can annihilate almost a square mile (2.5 sq km) of terrain

The AGM-86 is an air-launched cruise missile usually deployed by a B-52 Stratofortress. A B-52H can carry a maximum of 20 such weapons. Once launched, the AGM-86 uses its onboard Global Positioning System (GPS) technology to fly itself to the target.

with up to 50,000 lb (22,680 kg) of bombs in a single pass. The B2 "Stealth Bomber" has all the stealth properties of the F-117, but is capable of dropping nuclear weapons or 24,000 lb (10,890 kg) of conventional explosive. (It is also the most expensive aircraft ever made, each one costing over $1 billion.) What such weapons ensure is that the USAF can handle any threat or challenge and totally dominate the airspace.

Maintaining and developing such a cutting-edge military force does not come cheap. The current military budget for the U.S. Air Force is around $100 billion, making it the most expensive of the four U.S. armed services.

SURVEILLANCE AND ELECTRONIC DEFENSE

The USAF is watching the world 24 hours a day. Surveillance satellites, reconnaissance aircraft, and sophisticated radar provide the United States with an accurate picture of what potentially hostile nations are doing.

Accurate surveillance is vital for all military operations. One of the best examples of this occurred in the Gulf War (1990–1991). At the beginning of the war, the biggest threat to U.S. and Allied aircraft was Iraq's extensive radar system. Iraq had a massive system of surface-to-air missiles (SAMs), each missile controlled by a network of targeting radars threaded throughout Iraq and occupied Kuwait. If the Allies were to achieve air superiority, this radar system had to be taken out.

To accomplish this, USAF Grumman/General Dynamics EF-111A Ravens and U.S. Navy/Marine Corps Grumman EA-6B Prowlers flew surveillance missions over Iraq and plotted almost all enemy radar systems. One particularly clever technique used by the USAF was to send large flights of jets toward the Iraqi border,

Left: The SR-71 Blackbird served from 1964 to 1998 as a high-altitude reconnaissance aircraft. Blackbirds were capable of flying at speeds of more than 2,200 mph (3,540 km/h) and at heights of around 85,000 ft (27,880 m).

An EC-130 Compass Call aircraft on patrol during the Gulf War. The EC-130 is a modified C-130 Hercules transport aircraft packed with electronic countermeasures. It is operated by a crew of 13 specialists who constantly monitor and block enemy communications.

prompting the SAM operators to turn on all their radar systems. As soon as they were turned on, the U.S. jets turned around and flew back to safety, while the surveillance aircraft quickly plotted every single SAM position by using the targeting signals. Once a full picture was built up about Iraqi command-and-control systems, U.S. and British warplanes flew in and fired antiradar missiles to wipe out the targets. Those Iraqi radar positions that were not destroyed had their signals jammed by USAF Lockheed EC-130H Compass Call aircraft, which carry the ALQ-99 Tactical Jamming System on board. Iraq found itself completely blind, unable to monitor or detect enemy forces. By contrast, the USAF was able to watch Iraqi ground and air forces around the clock.

SURVEILLANCE TECHNOLOGIES

The USAF has three main types of surveillance technology: airborne surveillance, ground-based radar, and satellite surveillance. This chapter will examine the first technology—satellite and radar surveillance is described in the next chapter.

THE U-2 INCIDENT

In the 1950s, the USAF's main high-altitude surveillance aircraft was the U-2. This amazing aircraft could fly at an altitude of 75,000 ft (24,600 m). Even at that altitude, its onboard cameras were capable of photographing a golf ball on a putting green. Between 1955 and 1960, U-2s conducted regular surveillance missions over the Soviet Union, high above enemy SAMs. However, in the late 1950s, the Soviet Union acquired the high-altitude SAM-2 weapon, and on May 1, 1960, a U-2 flown by USAF pilot Gary Powers was shot down. The United States faced a delicate situation. Powers was captured, but President Eisenhower initially denied that the aircraft was flying in Soviet airspace. Then on May 7, 1960, the Soviet leader Khrushchev announced to the world what had happened and that Powers had been captured. There followed many weeks of difficult negotiations. The Soviets argued that the United States was jeopardizing any chances of peace, while the United States defended itself by saying that it needed to patrol Soviet skies to guard against a surprise attack with nuclear weapons. After the U-2 incident, the United States stopped flying high-altitude missions over the Soviet Union.

The U.S. Air Force has the most advanced aerial surveillance vehicles in the world. They serve four main purposes: gathering intelligence and surveillance; assisting communications between military units; providing countermeasures against enemy radar and intelligence; and assisting in defining targets for Army, Navy, or Air Force weaponry. Two exceptional aircraft in particular are used in almost every conflict or peacekeeping mission of U.S. forces: the E-3 Sentry Airborne Warning and Control System (AWACS) and the E-8C Joint STARS. Each performs distinct roles, and together they give U.S. forces an eagle-eye view of the battlefield.

E-3 Sentry AWACS aircraft have been used constantly since the early 1990s. During Operation Desert Shield in the Gulf War, E-3s flew 24 hours a day, giving Allied aircraft the information needed to fly 120,000 sorties and destroy 38 Iraqi aircraft in the air. The E-3 is actually a converted civil airliner, the Boeing 707. The most striking feature of the conversion is a massive radar dome stuck on top of the **fuselage**—30 ft (9.1 m) in diameter, 6 ft (1.8 m) thick, and supported 14 ft (4.2 m) above the fuselage. This radar is a probing, long-range surveillance instrument. It can scan for enemy ships, vehicles, and aircraft, scanning out to a distance of more than 250 miles (375.5 km) and from an altitude of over 9 miles (15 km). The radar has another feature, called identification friend or foe (IFF), which automatically tells the crew if the object detected on the radar is allied or enemy.

Inside the E-3 are banks of computer consoles manned by up to 19 specialist communication officers (there are also four flight crew). All information gathered from the radar and other sources is

A devastated Iraqi column after an Allied air strike. USAF satellite and air surveillance meant that Iraqi vehicles could not move without having their positions monitored and tracked. With nowhere to hide, they were easy victims for USAF strike aircraft.

presented on these computers. The information is then transferred to allied command-and-control systems on the ground and in the air via a Joint Tactical Information Distribution System (JTIDS), which is secure from enemy attempts to hack into allied communications. In addition to surveillance, the E-3 is also fitted with Global Positioning System (GPS) technology, which lets it give the exact coordinates of enemy forces to allied troops. All this

This view of an E-3 Sentry AWACS clearly shows its 30-ft (9.1-m) radar dome on top of the fuselage. In the Gulf War, Sentry aircraft provided control for over 120,000 allied combat missions.

technology is expensive, however—each Sentry aircraft costs an enormous $123.4 million.

While the E-3 Sentry conducts surveillance of land, sea, and air, the E-8C Joint Surveillance Targets Attack Radar System (Joint STARS) is focused on detecting enemy armor on the ground. The

E-8C, like the E-3, was developed during the 1980s and first deployed in the Gulf War. During its early operations, E-8Cs detected, monitored, and plotted hundreds of Iraqi tanks and mobile missile launches, most of which were then destroyed by allied strike-aircraft using the E-8C's information.

Again, the E-8C is a modified Boeing 707, but unlike the E-3, its main radar is housed in a 40-ft (12-m) long tube attached beneath the fuselage. This radar can detect vehicles moving within an area of 19,305 square miles (50,000 sq km), and track multiple targets simultaneously. Its moving target indicator (MTI) and fixed target indicator (FTI) can distinguish between static and mobile targets, and this information is relayed in "real time" to Army ground stations. "Real time" surveillance means that the information is updated almost every second. E-8Cs can control attacks from infantry, artillery, naval gunfire, and attack aircraft, and in the Gulf War, it had a 100 percent success rate in detecting enemy vehicles and facilitating their destruction. Each E-8C costs a huge $244.4 million and carries four flight crew and 18 onboard specialists.

UNMANNED AERIAL VEHICLES

The Air Force currently has entire squadrons of aircraft with one unusual feature—they have no pilots. These aircraft are known as Unmanned Aerial Vehicles (UAVs), and they may represent the future of air warfare and surveillance. UAVs are aircraft that are flown not by a pilot who sits on board, but by a controller who stays on the ground and flies the aircraft by remote control. Information from the UAV's onboard cameras and sensors is fed back to the

Inside an E-8C Joint STARS surveillance aircraft up to 17 Air Force and Army operators use the sophisticated onboard radar to detect, identify, and track up to 1,000 moving targets. The information is then relayed to attack aircraft or ground forces.

controller, providing all the information needed to fly the aircraft successfully and respond to any unexpected events. UAVs have some amazing advantages over piloted aircraft. They are over 50 percent cheaper to build than piloted aircraft; they can make maneuvers that would render a human pilot unconscious through the effects of G-force; training its controller is far quicker; no personnel are put at risk; and they can fly for hours on end, avoiding the problem of a pilot getting tired or needing to land.

This last virtue has made them ideal for use as surveillance aircraft. One of the most important UAVs currently in service is the RQ-1 Predator. The Predator is 27 ft (8.22 m) long, flies at only 140 mph (225 km/h), and can remain flying over a surveillance area for 16 hours before it has to return to base. On board the Predator is a color camera in the nose of the aircraft that provides the controller with sight, a high-power camera for daytime surveillance, an infrared camera for night-time/low-light operations, and a synthetic aperture radar that can look through smoke or clouds. Any information the Predator gathers is fed back to a ground-control station, which in turn transmits it to attack forces via a satellite-link communication suite. As of this writing, Predators are currently in use over Afghanistan as part of the war against terrorism, and they

The RQ-1 Predator Unmanned Aerial Vehicle (UAV) is the first of the USAF's pilotless aircraft. The "R" stands for "reconnaissance," the "Q" is the designation for "unmanned aircraft system," and the "1" indicates that it is the first of its type.

ELECTRONIC DEFENSE—THE EC-130H COMPASS CALL IN THE GULF WAR

Electronic intelligence (ELINT) and aerial surveillance were vital in winning the Gulf War. Equally vital were the efforts of the USAF to degrade and diminish the Iraqi forces' powers of communication. The USAF EC-130H Compass Call aircraft has been described as "Saddam's earache." With only nine such communications-jamming aircraft, the USAF seriously affected the operational ability of Iraq's military forces. Flying almost 24 hours a day, the EC-130Hs monitored Iraqi airwaves until they picked up communications between enemy units. They then had two options—either record the message for analysis by allied intelligence, or jam the communications. The jamming programs had an instant effect. Iraqi radio operators found their headphones filled with screeching and wailing sounds, and were unable to get rid of them. This disrupted Iraqi communications and so reduced their military effectiveness. In addition, Compass Call flights sometimes carried Iraqi-speaking operators on board, who would relay fake commands to enemy units, leading them into ambushes or air strikes. The efforts of Compass Call flights, and the quick responses of Allied attack aircraft, meant that in only six days, Iraqi SAM batteries suffered a 95 percent reduction in activity.

have provided invaluable information about enemy movements without risk to human pilots. The USAF is also successfully experimenting with arming Predators with Hellfire antitank

The Global Hawk UAV has no pilot, and so operates with incredible endurance. In 2001, a Global Hawk successfully completed an exercise in which it flew 7,500 miles (12,069 km) nonstop across the Pacific, from the U.S. to Australia.

missiles, giving UAVs the capability to operate as attack aircraft.

The other main UAV is the Global Hawk. This is a larger vehicle than the Predator, but it has a range of over 13,800 miles (22,208 km) and can fly at altitudes of up to 65,000 ft (19,812 m). Using the sophisticated Synthetic Aperture Radar/Ground Moving Target Indicator, it can plot every target in an area the size of Illinois (46,000 sq m/119,094 km) in only 24 hours.

It can remain flying over the battlefield (known as being "in station") for 24 hours—and this after flying a distance of up to 1,200 miles (1,931 km) to the surveillance area. Global Hawk is also being armed, and the future of aerial warfare seems deeply involved with the development of UAVs.

WOODEN STAKE
SPACECRAFT

U.S.
AIR FORCE

USAF

MDAC

DELTA
II

THE U.S. AIR FORCE IN SPACE

The U.S. Air Force is active hundreds of miles above the earth's surface. Its Air Force Space Command explores the opportunities that space presents for the defensive and offensive capabilities of the United States.

Air Force Space Command (AFSPC) was created on September 1, 1982. It is possibly the most powerful command of any branch of the U.S. military because it maintains and operates all U.S. nuclear intercontinental ballistic missiles (ICBMs). Day and night, it monitors the entire world and acts as a real deterrent to aggressive nations possibly using nuclear weapons against the United States.

AFSPC has many other duties besides operating its nuclear arsenal. It launches military and navigational satellites into space. It monitors space itself, plotting the positions and behavior of non-U.S. space vehicles and potentially dangerous space debris. Its satellite systems provide weather information, worldwide communications, missile warnings, and navigational systems to soldiers on the ground. With over 33,000 people employed in these roles, AFSPC is a vital organization for U.S. defense.

Left: Air Force Space Command satellites perform one of four functions: Global Positioning System (GPS) navigation, meteorological surveillance, defense surveillance and early warning, and satellite communications. They are launched by Atlas II, Delta II, Titan II, or Titan IV launch vehicles.

The Minuteman III intercontinental ballistic missiles are the latest in a series of missiles developed from the late 1950s. They are launched from silos located at USAF bases in Wyoming, Montana, and Nevada and are controlled by two-man launch crews.

NUCLEAR FORCE AND DETECTION

U.S. ICBM defenses are effectively run by two units: the 14th Air Force, based at Vandenberg AFB, California, and the 90th Space Wing at Warren AFB, Wyoming. The 14th Air Force controls a network of Defense Support Program (DSP) satellites, which monitor the Earth from a distance of 22,000 miles (35,404 km), using infrared detectors to look for any sign of missile launches. Each DSP satellite contains over 2,000 detectors, and all data they

Since the 1960s, the USAF has been monitoring the world for signs of hostile missile launches. Early-warning crews are maintained at a 100 percent alert status—they are fully prepared to respond to nuclear attack at any time night or day.

receive is passed on to North American Air Defense Command (NORAD) and USSPACECOM early-warning centers at Cheyenne Mountain, Colorado, and to National Command Authorities. The 90th Space Wing is responsible for operating U.S. ICBM weapon systems themselves, such as the Minuteman and Peacemaker missiles. It is an elite unit, and remains in a state of over 99 percent readiness—which simply means that it is always prepared to respond within minutes to any nuclear threat. U.S. nuclear forces have maintained a 24-hour alert since 1959. The United States currently has over 500 ICBMs in its weaponry. All of them are contained in reinforced-concrete launch silos situated beneath the Great Plains.

DSP satellites are eventually to be surpassed by the Space-Based Infrared System (SBIRS) system. The SBIRS will contain around 30 satellites to give extremely precise coordinates of any missile launch, a faster report time to commanders back in the United States, and more accurate prediction of where the missile will land. But satellites are not the only systems of monitoring the world for missile launches. The USAF also operates a network of ground-based early-warning radars in the United States and abroad. The most sophisticated of these is the PAVE PAWS radar system, which not only tracks earth-orbiting satellites, but can also simultaneously detect and monitor hundreds of missiles if they are launched.

To defend against such an attack, the USAF is developing laser-defense systems. These are powerful laser weapons that will be deployed in orbiting satellites to destroy enemy ICBMs as they fly through space and the Earth's atmosphere. Based on current Space-

An artist's impression of the theoretical "Brilliant Pebbles" space-based missile-defense system. Over 4,600 small interceptors would be deployed in orbit, each capable of detecting and destroying an enemy nuclear missile using kinetic-energy weapons.

Based Laser (SBL) technology, the time from detection of missile to its destruction would be only 1–10 seconds. The first SBL weapons should be ready for service over the next few years and will throw a protective shield across the entire United States.

SATELLITE AND SURVEILLANCE SUPPORT

The AFSPC is not just concerned with nuclear defense. It also deploys, operates, and monitors a range of satellite services, without which the U.S. military would be severely weakened. Possibly the

General Richard B. Meyers of the U.S. Air Force speaks to reporters on the activities of the U.S. Space Command at a Pentagon briefing, January 2000.

most important is the Navstar Global Positioning Satellite (GPS) system. The GPS system consists of 24 satellites, each of which orbits the Earth every 12 hours, emitting continuous navigation signals. Military and civilian personnel on the ground use a special receiver to receive these signals, determining their exact coordinates to an accuracy of within 100 ft (33 m). GPS is now absolutely essential for military operations. Army, Navy, and Air Force navigators rely on GPS to plot their positions, and many precision-guided missiles and bombs now use GPS to guide them to their targets.

In addition to GPS, AFSPC serves the military community by providing the Defense Satellite Communications System (DSCS). Ten Phase III DSCS satellites orbit the Earth at an altitude of 23,000 miles (37,013 km). They provide secure worldwide communications for all U.S. military forces, and they are totally resistant to any attempts to jam them. The DSCS satellites are also part of the U.S. early-warning system, and every day, confidential information flits around the world at lightning speed. Another more advanced communications system is the Milstar, which is described as a "smart switchboard." The Milstar not only enables voice communications, but can also transfer encrypted voice, data, Teletype, or facsimile communications safe from prying eyes.

Not all frontline AFSPC technology is based in space. One important role based on land is the Ground-Base Electro-Optical Deep-Space Surveillance (GEODSS) unit, which has its headquarters in the U.S. Space Command's Space Control Center in Cheyenne Mountain Air Force Station, Colorado Springs, Colorado. Using a mixture of telescopes, low-light level television cameras, radars, and advanced computers, GEODSS tracks some of the more than 10,000 objects that orbit the Earth. Most of these objects are manmade, such as satellites or pieces of debris from space vehicles that have broken up, but GEODSS also tracks potentially hazardous meteors and comets. The GEODSS telescopes are so sensitive that they can monitor objects 10,000 times dimmer than the dimmest object visible to the human eye. By tracking such objects, GEODSS is able to protect the United States from space objects suddenly entering the Earth's atmosphere.

THE CUBAN MISSILE CRISIS

In 1962, the world came the closest it has ever done to nuclear war. The United States and the Soviet Union were locked in a nuclear arms race, and the Soviets were losing. Although U.S. missiles could easily reach the Soviet Union, **Communist** nuclear weapons could reach only as far as Europe. The Soviet solution was to construct nuclear-missile launch facilities on the Communist island of Cuba, only a few hundred miles from the U.S. coast. On October 15, 1962, President John F. Kennedy was informed of this construction—and took swift action.

A ring of Navy ships and USAF aircraft was thrown around Cuba, stopping Soviet ships from bringing in more missiles. Kennedy also demanded the removal of all existing missiles. Tensions began to build as Soviet and U.S. Navy ships faced each other, preparing for battle. On October 27, a U-2 reconnaissance aircraft was shot down over Cuba, and for 24 hours, the world feared it would be plunged into nuclear war. At the last minute, President Kennedy and the Soviet leader, Nikita Khrushchev, reached an agreement. The Soviet Union agreed to remove its missiles from Cuba, and the United States promised not to invade the island. The entire world breathed a sigh of relief.

Right: The leader of Cuba during the time of the Cuban Missile Crisis was Fidel Castro. Castro led a guerrilla army during the 1950s and overthrew the Cuban government in 1959 to become prime minister.

OPERATIONS AROUND THE WORLD

Within a year of its formation, the USAF was performing its first major operation—airlifting supplies into Berlin, West Germany, in defiance of the Communist blockade around the city.

At the end of World War II, Germany was split into two halves. The United States and the Allies controlled the western half; the eastern half was under the jurisdiction of the Communist Soviet Union. Although Germany's capital, Berlin, was set in the Russian sector, the city itself was divided into two halves controlled by the opposing sides. Russia and the United States had been allies during the war, but the end of the war emphasized the differences in their ideology and politics, and the former allies became committed enemies.

In June 1948, the Soviets suddenly announced that they were closing U.S. road and rail access routes to Berlin, thereby effectively placing the entire city under Communist control. The United States was faced with a choice: either abandon the city to the Soviets or attempt to use three air corridors to supply West Berlin with all the essentials of living. They chose the second option, and the USAF was called into action.

The airlift was known as Operation Vittles, and was one of the

Left: An aircraft is loaded with Sidewinder missiles during Operation Deny Flight, 1993. Deny Flight lasted from April 1993 to December 1995. Its mission was to stop hostile aircraft from flying over Bosnia-Herzegovina in the former Yugoslavia.

biggest rescue operations in history. On June 26, 1948, USAF C-47 Dakota aircraft flew 80 tons of supplies into Berlin's Templehof Airport. Eighty tons only scratched the surface of what was actually needed, but soon more USAF aircraft and airplanes from the U.S. Navy and British Royal Air Force were helping out. Meanwhile, three USAF bomber groups were sent into the area to provide nuclear deterrence against the Soviets.

Soon, the airlift had reached the stage of landing one aircraft every three minutes, bringing in the 4,500 tons of food, fuel, and other necessities that kept West Berlin alive. There were many dangers, however. Although the Communists did not fire on any of the aircraft, they harassed them by shining intense searchlights at them, jamming their radio communications, and "buzzing" them with fighter aircraft. Because of these efforts, and the dangers of such crowded airspace, 31 U.S. personnel and 34 Allied personnel were killed during the 11-month airlift. Their heroic missions, however, stopped half a city from starving, and on May 12, 1949, the Soviets finally backed down, reopening U.S. and British land routes into the city.

The Berlin airlift was the USAF's first major operation, but it showed the world how significant U.S. military aviation had become. Since World War II, there have been few years in which the USAF has not been involved with major military or humanitarian missions. Between 1945 and the mid-1980s, most of these operations were in the context of the Cold War. In the Korean War (1950–1953) and the Vietnam War (1963–1975), USAF units were deployed in force to fight major conflicts and attempt to stop the

The USAF flew more than 4,500 tons of supplies into Berlin between June 1948 and May 1949 after the city was cut off by the Russians. Here, the crew of the last USAF aircraft to fly into the city ironically advertise their "slightly used aircraft for sale."

spread of Communism in the Far East. Since the 1980s, USAF operations have been more concerned with fighting terrorism, controlling aggressive regimes, and performing hundreds of rescue and emergency airlifts. This chapter will look at two major conflicts in which the USAF made its presence felt: the Vietnam War and the Persian Gulf War.

THE VIETNAM WAR (1963–1975)

Actual fighting between North Vietnam and the United States did not begin until 1964, but the United States had been involved in protecting South Vietnam from Communist takeover since the 1950s. In 1961, USAF and U.S. Army personnel were deployed in South Vietnam to train South Vietnamese military forces to resist the Communist **guerrillas**. The USAF was there just to advise, but it was still dangerous work. Soon, four U.S. Army helicopters had been shot down by the Viet Cong, and USAF aircraft were also targeted. Between 1962 and 1964, the USAF gradually played a more active role. Transport aircraft dropped flares over the Vietnamese jungles to expose enemy units, and surveillance aircraft conducted reconnaissance on behalf of the South Vietnamese Army.

Everything changed on August 2, 1964. North Vietnamese torpedo boats attacked the USS *Maddox* floating in the South China Sea, and further attacks against U.S. shipping occurred over the next two nights. In response, the President authorized the use of air strikes against North Vietnam in retaliation. It was the beginning of the air war.

During 1964, most USAF and U.S. Navy air strikes were in retaliation to attacks on U.S. personnel or installations. However, in 1965, U.S. combat troops were officially deployed in South Vietnam, and the USAF unleashed its full power in Operation Rolling Thunder. Rolling Thunder ran from February 1965 until October 1968, and was one of the heaviest bombing campaigns of all history. The operation involved a sustained bombing of North Vietnam, with the intention of forcing them to give up their military action in South Vietnam. Over three years, USAF, U.S. Navy, and U.S. Marine Corps aircraft dropped over one million tons of bombs on North Vietnam.

The main USAF aircraft used in Rolling Thunder were McDonnell Douglas F-4 Phantoms, Republic F-105 Thunderchiefs, North American F-100 Super Sabers, and Douglas A-4 Skyhawks. All were excellent ground-attack aircraft, and they were put to work demolishing key targets in North Vietnam. These targets included bridges, roads, railroad depots, oil-storage tanks, steelworks, airfields,

A Cessna A-37B Dragonfly fires its rockets into the Vietnamese jungle in 1967. U.S. ground troops in Vietnam relied heavily on air strikes, because it was often difficult to have visual contact with the enemy when on the ground.

military bases, communications centers, vital roads, and North Vietnamese supply routes into South Vietnam. Initially, they faced only unsophisticated North Vietnamese machine guns and antiaircraft guns. By 1967, however, North Vietnam had received huge numbers of the modern Soviet SA-2 Guideline SAMs, which were radar-guided and could hit aircraft at up to 69,000 ft (21,000 m). U.S. pilots often faced a new missile attack every few seconds, and had to throw their aircraft madly around the sky in an attempt to shake off the supersonic missiles.

Rolling Thunder was a massive bombardment, but it did not have its intended effect. Although 52,000 North Vietnamese were killed, the bombing did not stop supplies from getting through to the North Vietnamese in South Vietnam. So on October 31, 1968, President Johnson ordered the operation to stop.

USAF operations continued after Rolling Thunder. The Air Force was used mainly to attack Communist units operating in the South Vietnamese jungles and Communist supply routes into South Vietnam through neighboring Laos.

In 1973, all U.S. combat troops on the ground were withdrawn from Vietnam, but the USAF remained to assist South Vietnamese operations until 1975. They were unable to stop the tide of Communism from flooding over into South Vietnam, but they did gain huge amounts of combat experience and had demonstrated the power of their technology.

The defeat in Vietnam left all U.S. military forces hugely demoralized. However, in 1990, an operation began that, in the words of President George Bush, Sr., "laid to rest the ghosts of Vietnam."

GULF WAR (1990–1991)

On August 2, 1990, the military forces of Iraq invaded and occupied neighboring Kuwait. This action set alarm bells ringing around the world. Kuwait and its neighbor, Saudi Arabia, were important oil-producing nations, and it looked as if Iraq, led by President Saddam Hussein, was eyeing Saudi Arabia as the next conquest. In response, the United States led a coalition of military forces, which were sent to Saudi Arabia as part of Operation Desert Shield. Their mission: to protect Saudi Arabia at all costs.

USAF COMBAT CONTROLLERS

Combat controllers are the unseen warriors of the U.S. Air Force. Their job is to penetrate deep behind enemy lines and pick out targets for destruction by USAF attack aircraft, to conduct rescue operations for downed U.S. pilots, and to act as on-the-ground air traffic controllers for U.S. aircraft. Only 350 combat controllers are qualified, and their training standards are as high, if not higher, than any elite force in the Army or Navy. They are fully trained in combat, surveillance, covert operations, rescue, combat medicine, and airborne and amphibious deployments, as well as a whole range of other skills. Basic training lasts up to a year, and a typical training exercise involves a three-mile (4.8-km) run followed by a 4,573-ft (1,500-m) swim in uniform. Like the U.S. Navy SEALs, the USAF combat controllers can operate on land, sea, and in the air, and this elite force has been behind the success of many recent USAF missions.

The USAF responded with lightning speed. Only five days after the initial invasion of Kuwait, F-15C Eagle strike-aircraft from the 1st Tactical Fighter Wing, Langley AFB, Virginia, landed in Saudi Arabia, and they began flying defensive missions along the Iraqi border only three days later. By January 1991, more than 2,000 U.S. aircraft had been moved into the region. While Desert Shield was in place, Iraq was given an ultimatum: withdraw from Kuwait or face the full might of U.S. and Allied military forces. Saddam Hussein did not respond, and on January 17, 1991, Operation Desert Shield was replaced by Operation Desert Storm.

Once the decision to fight had been made, the USAF and other air forces set to work devastating the Iraqi war machine, one of the most powerful in the Middle East. The first aircraft into action were B-52Gs Stratofortresses, flying from Barksdale AFB in the United States, and F-117 Stealth fighters. The B-52s fired AGM-86C air-launched cruise missiles at key targets within Iraq, while the F-117s flew inside Iraq and smashed radar, air defenses, and communications systems. Soon, the full might of the USAF was brought to bear against the Iraqi forces. Iraqi troops and military vehicles inside Iraq and Kuwait were undoubtedly the hardest hit. Night and day, USAF aircraft pounded troop positions with B-52 bombers or strike aircraft, using precision-guided munitions to wreck tanks, trucks, missile launchers, and other tools of transportation. In addition, Iraq's radar and communications system was almost entirely destroyed. The results of this horrific onslaught were evident when on February 24, 1991, Allied ground forces invaded Kuwait to expel the Iraqi occupiers. They won the battle in only 100 hours. They

Four 1,000-lb (453-kg) bombs fall from an F-16 on a training exercise at Nellis Air Force Base, Nevada. USAF aircraft in the Gulf War dropped or fired over 160,000 individual weapons and flew 38,000 combat sorties.

were able to do so because USAF and Allied airpower had destroyed 60 percent of Iraqi tanks, 40 percent of other armored vehicles, and 60 percent of its artillery. The Iraqi air force lost 234 airplanes. In total, the USAF lost only 13 aircraft.

USAF operations continue to this day over Iraq. Operations Southern Watch and Northern Watch are in force to stop Iraqi aircraft from flying over southern and northern Iraq and threatening their neighbors. F-15 and F-16 jets have had to engage Iraqi SAM batteries on many occasions, and the missions over Iraq remain dangerous ones for the USAF.

RECENT OPERATIONS

Since the Gulf War, the USAF has rarely been out of action. In 1992, civil war broke out in Yugoslavia, as the country fragmented into different ethnic and geographical groups. Sarajevo, the capital of Bosnia-Herzegovina (a territory within Yugoslavia), was completely under siege from Bosnians allied with neighboring Serbia. The city was pounded by artillery, and food was running out. In Operation Provide Promise, the USAF flew essential humanitarian supplies into the city. The operation lasted for three and a half years, one of the longest airlift operations in history.

Serbia tried to stop the rescue mission with all their means. USAF aircraft were fired upon, and an Italian transport aircraft was

Captain Scott F. O'Grady with President Bill Clinton on June 12, 1995. Captain O'Grady was being welcomed home after being shot down in the former Yugoslavia and surviving for six days behind enemy lines.

shot down and its crew killed. In response, the USAF and NATO allies began a month-long bombing campaign against Serbia in August 1995. The Serbian capital, Belgrade, and most of its utilities and industry were bombed, the intention being to get the population to put pressure on the government to stop the war. It worked. On November 1, 1995, peace talks began, and these led to a stoppage of aggressive military actions by Serbia and other regions.

Unfortunately, violence flared up again in the region in 1998, this time in the country of Kosovo. Kosovan Serbians and Serbian military forces began to expel or murder ethnic Albanian civilians from the country—Kosovo's population is made up of many people formerly from neighboring Albania. Over 800,000 refugees poured over the border into Albania. Once again, the USAF under NATO command was called into action. U.S. strike-aircraft hunted down Serbian vehicles and troops and bombed them on the ground, while other aircraft hit Belgrade with cruise missiles and precision-guided munitions. Again, the bombing worked, and eventually Serbian forces withdrew from Kosovo.

The latest USAF mission is Operation Enduring Freedom, the war against terrorism that is the response to attacks against the U.S. on September 11, 2001. USAF bombing missions from B-52 and B-1 bombers have devastated Taliban fighting positions in Afghanistan. Other Taliban and Al Qaeda soldiers holding out in the mountains have suffered tremendous losses from U.S. C-130 aircraft deploying 15,000-lb (6,804-kg) BLU-82 blast bombs. The war against terrorism is far from over, and no doubt the USAF will find itself used in many other combat and humanitarian missions.

GLOSSARY

Airship: a lighter-than-air aircraft having propulsion and steering systems

Biplane: an aircraft with two main supporting surfaces, usually placed one above the other

Cold War: a state of hostilities short of outright war that existed from 1945 to the late 1980s between the Communist Soviet Union and the United States and its allies

Communism: a totalitarian system of government in which a single authoritarian party controls state-owned means of production

Contingency operations: operations of a short duration and most often performed at short notice, such as dropping supplies into a combat zone

Covert: secret; veiled

Cruise missile: a missile programmed to fly like an aircraft to its target

Depleted uranium: one of the hardest known substances, it has most of its radioactivity removed before being used to make bullets

Fuselage: the central body portion of an aircraft designed to accommodate the crew and the passengers or cargo

G-force: a term used in the USAF to refer to the force of gravity imposed on a pilot during maneuvers; "2G," for example, means twice the force of gravity

Guerrilla: a person who engages in irregular warfare, especially as a member of an independent unit carrying out harassment and sabotage

Infiltration: the act of entering or becoming established in a group gradually or unobtrusively, usually for subversive purposes

NATO: North Atlantic Treaty Organization, an organization formed in 1949 and composed of European and North American states devoted to protecting their territories from Soviet threat

Sortie: one mission or attack by a single plane

Surveillance: to closely watch over and monitor situations; the USAF employs many different kinds of surveillance equipment and techniques in its role as an intelligence gatherer

Tactician: a person who employs forces in combat

CHRONOLOGY

1903: The Wright brothers make the world's first flight in a powered, heavier-than-air aircraft.

1907: August 1, U.S. Army Signal Corps forms an Aeronautical Division.

1913: The U.S. Army 1st Aero Squadron is operational.

1918: May 24, President Woodrow Wilson creates the Army Air Service in response to the growth of military air power during World War I.

1926: July 2, the Air Service is redesignated as the Army Air Corps.

1939–1945: The Second World War transforms U.S. military aviation.

1941: June 20, the United States Army Air Force (USAAF) is created and becomes the largest air force in the world by 1944.

1947: September 18, the United States Air Force (USAF) is formed, officially a separate unit from the U.S. Army; October 14, USAF test pilot Chuck Yeager flies his Bell XS-1 at more than the speed of sound, the world's first supersonic flight.

1961–1975: The USAF becomes involved in the Vietnam War; it loses over 2,000 aircraft during the conflict and conducts some of the heaviest bombing raids in history.

1980s: The USAF conducts regular military operations in several places, including Grenada (1983), Libya (1986), and Panama (1989).

1990–1991: The Gulf War; the USAF plays a dominant role in destroying Iraqi military forces and supporting Allied operations.

1992–1998: USAF combat aircraft and humanitarian flights perform hundreds of missions in the former Yugoslavia.

2001–: Following the attacks against the United States on September 11, the USAF conducts operations as part of the war against terrorism, particularly in Afghanistan.

FURTHER INFORMATION

USEFUL WEB SITES

The USAF's own Web site: www.af.mil/

For information about USAF careers, see: www.airforce.com/

For the USAF Museum: www.wpafb.af.mil/museum/

For the Air National Guard: www.ang.af.mil/

FURTHER READING

Archer, Robert J. *U.S. Air Force: A New Century*. Minnesota: North Branch, 2000.

Basel, G.I. *Pak Six: A Story of the War in the Skies of North Vietnam*. New York: Jove Publications, 1992.

Boyne, Walter J. *Beyond the Wild Blue: A History of the United States Air Force 1947–1997*. New York: St. Martins Press, 1997.

Brehm, Jack et.al. *That Others May Live: The True Story of the PJs, Real Life Heroes of the Perfect Storm*. New York: Three Rivers Press, 2001.

Donald, David, ed. *U.S. Air Force Air Power Directory*. Westport, Connecticut: Airtime Publishing, 1992.

Morse, Stan. *Gulf Air War Debrief*. Westport, Connecticut: Airtime Publishing, 1991.

U.S. Department of the Air Force Handbook. New York: International Business Publications, 2000.

ABOUT THE AUTHOR

Dr. Chris McNab has written and edited numerous books on military history and the world's elite military forces. His list of publications to date includes *The Illustrated History of the Vietnam War, German Paratroopers of World War II, The World's Best Soldiers, The Elite Forces Manual of Endurance Techniques,* and *How to Pass the SAS Selection Course.* Chris' research into these titles has brought him into contact with many of the world's elite units, including the U.S. Marines and British Special Forces. Chris has also contributed to the field of military technology with publications such as *Weapons of War: AK47, Twentieth-Century Small Arms,* and *Modern Military Uniforms.* His editorial projects include *The Battle of Britain* and *Fighting Techniques of the U.S. Marines 1941–45.* Chris lives in south Wales, U.K.

INDEX